God's Little Instruction Book for Graduates

HONOR BOOKS

Tulsa, Oklahoma

God's Little Instruction Book for Graduates — Special Edition
ISBN 1-56292-123-1
Copyright © 1994 by Honor Books, Inc.
P.O. Box 55388
Tulsa, Oklahoma 74155

$\mathcal{P}$resented To:

_____

$\mathcal{P}$resented By:

_____

$\mathcal{D}$ate

_____

INTRODUCTION

God's Little Instruction Book for Graduates is an inspirational collection of quotes and Scriptures that will motivate graduates from high school and college to live a meaningful, productive and happy life while inspiring them to strive for excellence and character in living.

We have combined man's greatest insights with the timeless wisdom of the Bible, covering topics that graduates everywhere can appreciate and learn more about. *God's Little Instruction Book for Graduates* will help graduates reach for excellence as they meet the challenges of the future.

When you were born, you cried and the world rejoiced. Live your life in such a manner that when you die the world cries and you rejoice.

The memory of the righteous will be a blessing....

Proverbs 10:7 NIV

*M*any receive advice, only the wise profit by it.

*Pride only breeds quarrels, but wisdom is found
in those who take advice.*

Proverbs 13:10 NIV

Even a mosquito doesn't get a slap on the back until it starts to work.

—•—

Work hard so God can say to you, "Well done."
Be a good workman, one who does not need to
be ashamed when God examines your work....

2 Timothy 2:15 TLB

You will never make a more important decision than the person you marry.

Therefore shall a man leave his father and his mother, and shall cleave unto his wife: and they shall be one flesh.

Genesis 2:24

The Bible has a word to describe "safe" sex: It's called marriage.

*Marriage should be honored by all,
and the marriage bed kept pure,
for God will judge the adulterer
and all the sexually immoral.*

Hebrews 13:4 NIV

*N*o horse gets anywhere
until he is harnessed.
No life ever grows great
until it is focused,
dedicated, disciplined.

In a race, everyone runs but only one person gets first prize....
To win the contest you must deny yourselves many things
that would keep you from doing your best.

1 Corinthians 9:24,25 TLB

I have never been hurt by anything I didn't say.

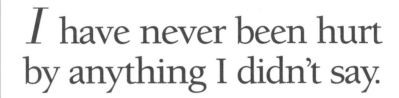

*Don't talk so much. You keep putting
your foot in your mouth.
Be sensible and turn off the flow!*

Proverbs 10:19 TLB

We too often love things and use people, when we should be using things and loving people.

Be devoted to one another in brotherly love.
Honor one another above yourselves.

Romans 12:10 NIV

*O*ne hundred years from now it won't matter if you got that big break, finally traded up to a Mercedes.... It will greatly matter, one hundred years from now, that you made a commitment to Jesus Christ.

For what is a man profited, if he shall gain the whole world, and lose his own soul?....

Matthew 16:26

*S*uccess is knowing
the difference between
cornering people
and getting them
in your corner.

Can two walk together, except they be agreed?

Amos 3:3

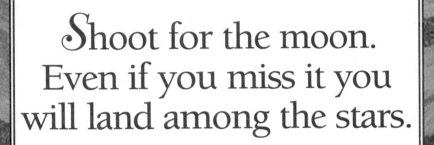

Shoot for the moon. Even if you miss it you will land among the stars.

Aim for perfection....
2 Corinthians 13:11 NIV

The secret of success is to do the common things uncommonly well.

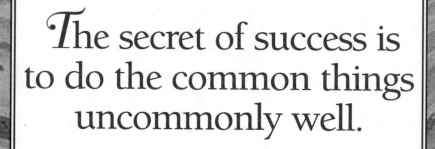

Seest thou a man diligent in his business? he shall stand before kings; he shall not stand before mean men.

Proverbs 22:29

Definition of status:
Buying something you
don't need with money
you don't have to impress
people you don't like.

But they do all their deeds to be noticed by men. . . .
Matthew 23:5 NASB

I like the dreams of the future better than the history of the past.

Remember ye not the former things, neither consider the things of old. Behold, I will do a new thing. . . .

Isaiah 43:18,19

The way to get to the top is to get off your bottom.

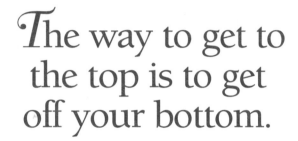

How long will you lie down, O sluggard?
When will you arise from your sleep?

Proverbs 6:9 NASB

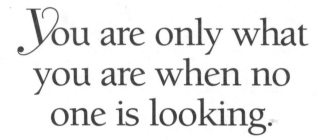

You are only what you are when no one is looking.

Not with eyeservice, as menpleasers;
but as the servants of Christ,
doing the will of God from the heart.

Ephesians 6:6

There are times when silence is golden, other times it is just plain yellow.

---

*To everything there is a season:. . .
a time to keep silence, and a time to speak.*

Ecclesiastes 3:1,7

Keep thy shop and thy shop will keep thee.

He who works his land will have abundant food,
but he who chases fantasies lacks judgement.

Proverbs 12:11 NIV

$\mathcal{E}$very job is a
self-portrait of the
person who does it.
Autograph your work
with excellence.

*Daniel was preferred above the presidents and princes,
because an excellent spirit was in him....*

Daniel 6:3

The best things in life are *not* free.

⊷•⊶

*Forasmuch as ye know that ye were not redeemed
with corruptible things, as silver and gold . . .
but with the precious blood of Christ
as of a lamb without blemish and without spot.*

1 Peter 1:18,19

You can lead a boy to college, but you cannot make him think.

*It is senseless to pay tuition to educate
a rebel who has no heart for truth.*

Proverbs 17:16 TLB

*I*f a man cannot be a Christian in the place where he is, he cannot be a Christian anywhere.

Don't work hard only when your master is watching and then shirk when he isn't looking; work hard and with gladness all the time, as though working for Christ, doing the will of God with all your hearts.

Ephesians 6:6,7 TLB

Don't ask God for what you think is good; ask Him for what He thinks is good for you.

After this manner therefore pray ye.... Thy kingdom come. Thy will be done in earth, as it is in heaven.

Matthew 6:9,10

Opportunities are seldom labeled.

*...Seek, and ye shall find; knock,
and it shall be opened unto you.*

Matthew 7:7

The wise does at once what the fool does at last.

*He that gathereth in summer is a wise son:
but he that sleepeth in harvest is
a son that causeth shame.*

Proverbs 10:5

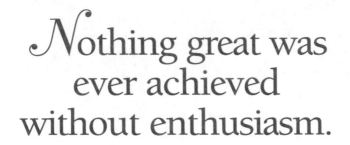

Nothing great was ever achieved without enthusiasm.

...For the joy of the LORD is your strength.
Nehemiah 8:10

Trust in yourself and you are doomed to disappointment; . . . but trust in God, and you are never to be confounded in time or eternity.

It is better to take refuge in the LORD than to trust in man.
Psalm 118:8 NIV

$\mathcal{D}$on't be discouraged; everyone who got where he is, started where he was.

Though your beginning was insignificant,
Yet your end will increase greatly.

Job 8:7 NASB

*M*aturity doesn't come
with age; it comes
with acceptance
of responsibility.

When I was a child, I spake as a child, I understood
as a child, I thought as a child: but when
I became a man, I put away childish things.

1 Corinthians 13:11

The man who wins may have been counted out several times, but he didn't hear the referee.

*For though a righteous man falls
seven times, he rises again....*

Proverbs 24:16 NIV

The happiest people
don't necessarily have
the best of everything.
They just make the
best of everything.

*...For I have learned, in whatsoever state
I am, therewith to be content. I can do all
things through Christ which strengtheneth me.*

Philippians 4:11,13

Keep company with good men and good men you will imitate.

Iron sharpeneth iron; so a man sharpeneth the countenance of his friend.

Proverbs 27:17

Learn by experience — preferably other people's.

All these things happened to them as examples – as object lessons to us – to warn us against doing the same things....

1 Corinthians 10:11 TLB

*I*t is not what a man
does that determines
whether his work
is sacred or secular,
it is why he does it.

Whatever you do, work at it with all your heart, as working for the Lord, not for men.... It is the Lord Christ you are serving.

Colossians 3:23,24 NIV

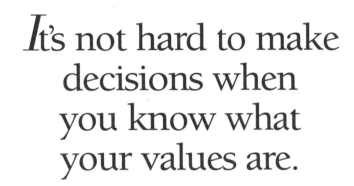

*I*t's not hard to make decisions when you know what your values are.

*But Daniel purposed in his heart that
he would not defile himself....*

Daniel 1:8

Conquer yourself rather than the world.

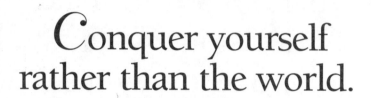

Similarly, encourage the young men to be self-controlled.

Titus 2:6 NIV

I am only one; but still
I am one. I cannot do
everything, but still I can
do something; I will not refuse
to do the something I can do.

———•———

Under his (Christ's) direction the whole body
is fitted together perfectly, and each part in its
own special way helps the other parts....

Ephesians 4:16 TLB

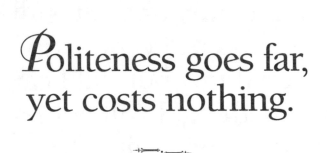

Politeness goes far, yet costs nothing.

A kind man benefits himself....
Proverbs 11:17 NIV

We should behave to our friends as we would wish our friends to behave to us.

And as ye would that men should do to you,
do ye also to them likewise.

Luke 6:31

The end must justify the means.

*The just man walketh in his integrity:
his children are blessed after him.*

Proverbs 20:7

Character is what you are in the dark.

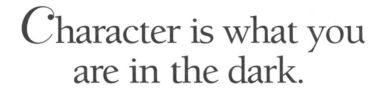

The integrity of the upright shall guide them....
Proverbs 11:3

Adversity causes some men to break; others to break records.

If thou faint in the day of adversity, thy strength is small.

Proverbs 24:10

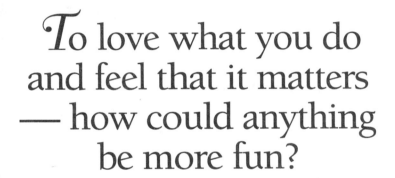

*T*o love what you do
and feel that it matters
— how could anything
be more fun?

... for my heart rejoiced in all my labour....
Ecclesiastes 2:10

A man who wants
to lead the orchestra
must turn his back
on the crowd.

*Wherefore come out from among them,
and be ye separate, saith the Lord, and touch
not the unclean thing; and I will receive you.*

2 Corinthians 6:17

*M*en are alike in their promises. It is only in their deeds that they differ.

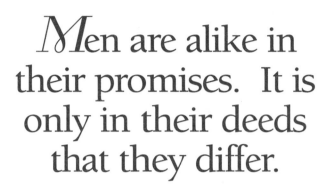

Many a man claims to have unfailing love,
but a faithful man who can find?

Proverbs 20:6 NIV

$\mathcal{D}$on't cross your bridges until you get to them. We spend our lives defeating ourselves crossing bridges we never get to.

So, don't be anxious about tomorrow. God will take care of your tomorrow too. Live one day at a time.

Matthew 6:34 TLB

*H*e that has learned to obey will know how to command.

The wise in heart accept commands,
but a chattering fool comes to ruin.

Proverbs 10:8 NIV

You must have long-range goals to keep you from being frustrated by short-range failures.

Let us fix our eyes on Jesus, the author and perfecter of our faith, who for the joy set before him endured the cross, scorning its shame, and sat down at the right hand of the throne of God.

Hebrews 12:2 NIV

Clear your mind of can't.

I can do all things through Christ which strengtheneth me.
Philippians 4:13

The future belongs to those who believe in the beauty of their dreams.

———

...anything is possible if you have faith.
Mark 9:23 TLB

The future belongs to those who see possibilities before they become obvious.

*For the vision is yet for an appointed time...
it will surely come, it will not tarry.*

Habakkuk 2:3

When I was a young man
I observed that nine out
of ten things I did were
failures. I didn't want to
be a failure, so I did
ten times more work.

*He becometh poor that dealeth with a slack hand:
but the hand of the diligent maketh rich.*

Proverbs 10:4

Luck is a matter of preparation meeting opportunity.

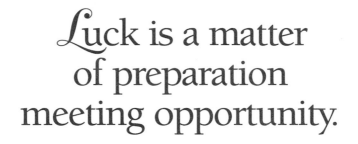

...make the most of every opportunity.

Colossians 4:5 NIV

Jumping to conclusions is not half as good an exercise as digging for facts.

Study to show thyself approved unto God, a workman that needeth not to be ashamed, rightly dividing the word of truth.

2 Timothy 2:15

The most valuable of all talents is that of never using two words when one will do.

In the multitude of words there wanteth not sin: but he that refraineth his lips is wise.

Proverbs 10:19

*L*aziness is often mistaken for patience.

...let us lay aside every weight, and the sin which doth so easily beset us, and let us run with patience the race that is set before us.

Hebrews 12:1

One-half the trouble of this life can be traced to saying yes too quick, and not saying no soon enough.

*Seest thou a man that is hasty in his words?
there is more hope of a fool than of him.*

Proverbs 29:20

I would rather fail in
the cause that someday
will triumph than
triumph in a cause
that someday will fail.

*Now thanks be unto God, which always
causeth us to triumph in Christ....*

2 Corinthians 2:14

Carve your name on hearts and not on marble.

⊢⟩⸱⟨⊣

The only letter I need is you yourselves! They can see that you are a letter from Christ written by us....not one carved on stone, but in human hearts.

2 Corinthians 3:2,3 TLB

A knowledge of the
Bible without a college
course is more valuable
than a college course
without the Bible.

*All scripture is given by inspiration of God, and is profitable
for doctrine, for reproof, for correction, for instruction
in righteousness: that the man of God may be perfect
thoroughly furnished unto all good works.*

2 Timothy 3:16,17

Little minds are tamed and subdued by misfortune; but great minds rise above them.

For a just man falleth seven times, and riseth up again....

Proverbs 24:16

There is no poverty that can overtake diligence.

—◄►•◄►—

He becometh poor that dealeth with a slack hand:
but the hand of the diligent maketh rich.

Proverbs 10:4

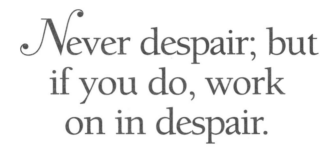

Never despair; but if you do, work on in despair.

But as for you, be strong and do not give up, for your work will be rewarded.

2 Chronicles 15:7 NIV

You can accomplish more in one hour with God than one lifetime without Him.

...With God all things are possible.
Matthew 19:26

*I*f you don't stand for something you'll fall for anything!

*...If you do not stand firm in your faith,
you will not stand at all.*

Isaiah 7:9 NIV

The difference
between ordinary
and extraordinary
is that little extra.

Whatsoever thy hand findeth to do, do it with thy might....
Ecclesiastes 9:10

*M*an cannot discover
new oceans unless he
has the courage to lose
sight of the shore.

*...and Peter got out of the boat, and walked
on the water and came toward Jesus.*

Matthew 14:29 NASB

*E*veryman is enthusiastic at times. One man has enthusiasm for thirty minutes, another has it for thirty days — but it is the man that has it for thirty years who makes a success in life.

———

...Let us run with perseverance the race marked out for us.

Hebrews 12:1 NIV

*P*erseverance is a great element of success; if you only knock long enough and loud enough at the gate you are sure to wake up somebody.

...Ask, and it shall be given you; seek, and ye shall find; knock, and it shall be opened unto you.

Luke 11:9

*C*onsider the postage
stamp: its usefulness
consists in the ability
to stick to one
thing till it gets there.

*I have fought a good fight, I have
finished my course, I have kept the faith.*
2 Timothy 4:7

*I*t needs more skill than I can tell To play the second fiddle well.

———

But he that is greatest among you shall be your servant.
Matthew 23:11

A man never discloses
his own character so
clearly as when he
describes another's.

*A good man out of the good treasure of the heart
bringeth forth good things; and an evil man out
of the evil treasure bringeth forth evil things.*

Matthew 12:35

The greatest use of life is to spend it for something that will outlast it.

———————

But store up for yourselves treasures in heaven,
where moth and rust do not destroy,
and where thieves do not break in and steal.

Matthew 6:20 NIV

*E*very man's work, whether
it be literature, or music,
or pictures, or architecture,
or anything else, is always
a portrait of himself.

As in water face reflects face, so the heart of man reflects man.

Proverbs 27:19 NASB

What we do on some great occasion will probably depend on what we already are; and what we are will be the result of previous years of self-discipline.

But I keep under my body, and bring it into subjection....
1 Corinthians 9:27

Our deeds determine us, as much as we determine our deeds.

Even a child is known by his actions, by whether his conduct is pure and right.

Proverbs 20:11 NIV

What you do speaks so loud that I cannot hear what you say.

...Show me your faith without deeds,
and I will show you my faith by what I do.

James 2:18 NIV

All virtue is summed up in dealing justly.

*He hath shewed thee, O man, what is good;
and what doth the LORD require of thee, but to do justly,
and to love mercy, and to walk humbly with thy God?*

Micah 6:8

No matter what a man's past may have been, his future is spotless.

*...Forgetting those things which are behind,
and reaching forth unto those things which are before.*

Philippians 3:13

One of life's great rules is this: the more you give, the more you get.

The liberal soul shall be made fat:
and he that watereth shall be watered also himself.

Proverbs 11:24,25

Everything comes to him who hustles while he waits.

We do not want you to become lazy, but to imitate those who through faith and patience inherit what has been promised.

Hebrews 6:12 NIV

A well-trained memory is one that permits you to forget everything that isn't worth remembering.

Finally, brethren, whatsoever things are true, whatsoever things are honest, whatsoever things are just...if there be any virtue, and if there be any praise, think on these things.

Philippians 4:8

Defeat is not the worst of failures. Not to have tried is the true failure.

Be strong and of a good courage; be not afraid, neither be thou dismayed: for the LORD thy God is with thee whithersoever thou goest.

Joshua 1:9

$\mathcal{U}$nless you try to do something beyond what you have already mastered, you will never grow.

*...reaching forth unto those things which
are before, I press toward the mark for the prize
of the high calling of God in Christ Jesus.*

Philippians 3:13,14

I don't know the secret to success but the key to failure is to try to please everyone.

Am I now trying to win the approval of man or of God?
Galatians 1:10 NIV

$\mathcal{K}$ites rise highest against the wind, not with it.

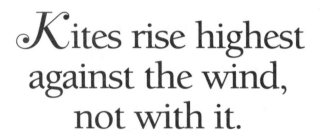

For when the way is rough, your patience has a chance to grow. So let it grow, and don't try to squirm out of your problems.

James 1:3,4 TLB

The Secret of success is to be like a duck — smooth and unruffled on top, but paddling furiously underneath.

...but I laboured more abundantly than they all: yet not I, but the grace of God which was with me.

1 Corinthians 15:10

... *T*he cheerful man will do more in the same time, will do it better, will preserve it longer, than the sad or sullen.

When a man is gloomy, everything seems to go wrong; when he is cheerful, everything seems right!

Proverbs 15:15 TLB

*M*oney is a good servant but a bad master.

The rich ruleth over the poor, and the borrower is servant to the lender.

Proverbs 22:7

*N*o plan is worth the paper it is printed on unless it starts you doing something.

But be ye doers of the word, and not hearers only, deceiving your own selves.

James 1:22

$\mathcal{L}$ife is a coin. You can spend it any way you wish, but you can spend it only once.

And as it is appointed unto men once to die, but after this the judgment.

Hebrews 12:2 NIV

Only passions, great passions, can elevate the soul to great things.

...fervent in spirit; serving the Lord.

Romans 12:11

*F*ailures want pleasing methods, successes want pleasing results.

⇥——•——⇤

No discipline seems pleasant at the time, but painful. Later on, however, it produces a harvest of righteousness and peace for those who have been trained by it.

Hebrews 12:11 NIV

Once a word has been allowed to escape, it cannot be recalled.

—————⊱•⊰—————

*Let no corrupt communication proceed out of your mouth,
but that which is good to the use of edifying, that it
may minister grace unto the hearers.*

Ephesians 4:29

*M*ost of the things worth doing in the world had been declared impossible before they were done.

...but with God all things are possible.
Matthew 19:26

Obstacles are those frightful things you see when you take your eyes off the goal.

So Peter...walked on the water toward Jesus. But when he looked around at the high waves, he was terrified and began to sink....

Matthew 14:29,30 TLB

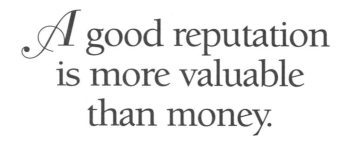

$\mathcal{A}$ good reputation is more valuable than money.

A good name is rather to be chosen than great riches....
Proverbs 22:1

An error doesn't become a mistake until you refuse to correct it.

*He who heeds discipline shows the way to life,
but whoever ignores correction leads others astray.*

Proverbs 10:17 NIV

*H*ating people is like burning down your own house to get rid of a rat.

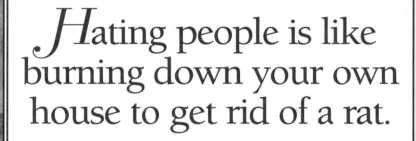

But if ye bite and devour one another, take heed that ye be not consumed one of another.

Galatians 5:15

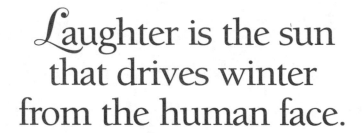

Laughter is the sun that drives winter from the human face.

A merry heart maketh a cheerful countenance:
but by sorrow of the heart the spirit is broken.

Proverbs 15:13

Good nature begets smiles, smiles beget friends, and friends are better than a fortune.

The light in the eyes (of him whose heart is joyful)
rejoices the heart of others....

Proverbs 15:30 AMP

No person was ever honored for what he received. Honor has been the reward for what he gave.

———

....the righteous give without sparing.
Proverbs 21:26 NIV

The difference between the right word and the almost right word is the difference between lightning and the lightning bug.

A word fitly spoken is like apples of gold in pictures of silver.
Proverbs 25:11

This world belongs
to the man who is
wise enough to
change his mind in
the presence of facts.

....whoever heeds correction gains understanding.
Proverbs 15:32 NIV

Blessed is the man who is too busy to worry in the daytime and too sleepy to worry at night.

The sleep of a labouring man is sweet....
Ecclesiastes 5:12

Every calling is great when greatly pursued.

*I press toward the mark for the prize
of the high calling of God in Christ Jesus.*

Philippians 3:14

*T*reat everybody alike,
no matter from what station
in life he comes....really great
men and women are those
who are natural, frank and
honest with everyone with
whom they come into contact.

...Don't show favoritism.
James 2:1 NIV

'Tis better to be alone, than in bad company.

Do not be misled: "Bad company corrupts good character."
1 Corinthians 15:33 NIV

The rotten apple spoils his companion.

He that walketh with wise men shall be wise:
but a companion of fools shall be destroyed.

Proverbs 13:20

Patience is bitter but its fruit is sweet.

———·———

For ye have need of patience, that, after ye have done the will of God, ye might receive the promise.

Hebrews 10:36

The greedy search for money or success will almost always lead men into unhappiness. Why? Because that kind of life makes them depend upon things outside themselves.

Let your character be free from the love of money, being content with what you have; for He Himself has said, "I will never desert you nor will I ever forsake you."

Hebrews 13:5 NASB

*N*ot only to say the right thing in the right place, but far more difficult, to leave unsaid the wrong thing at the tempting moment.

Self-control means controlling the tongue!
A quick retort can ruin everything.

Proverbs 13:3 TLB

School seeks to get you ready for examination; life gives the finals.

Examine yourselves to see whether you are in the faith; test yourselves.

2 Corinthians 13:5 NIV

$\mathcal{D}$iligence is the mother of good fortune.

—————

The plans of the diligent lead to profit....
Proverbs 21:5 NIV

The road to success is dotted with many tempting parking places.

...let us lay aside every weight, and the sin which doth so easily beset us, and let us run with patience the race that is set before us.

Hebrews 12:1

When you are laboring for others let it be with the same zeal as if it were for yourself.

Each of you should look not only to your own interests, but also to the interest of others.

Philippians 2:4 NIV

*T*he Bible knows nothing
of a hierarchy of labor.
No work is degrading.
If it ought to be done,
then it is good work.

...to rejoice in his labour; this is the gift of God.
Ecclesiastes 5:19

The ripest peach is highest on the tree.

*Let us not become weary in doing good, for at the proper
time we will reap a harvest if we do not give up.*

Galatians 6:9 NIV

When you do the things
you have to do when you
have to do them, the day
will come when you can do
the things you want to do
when you want to do them.

*He becometh poor that dealeth with a slack hand:
but the hand of the diligent maketh rich.*

Proverbs 10:4

A man without mirth
is like a wagon without
springs, he is jolted
disagreeably by every
pebble in the road.

A merry heart doeth good like a medicine:
but a broken spirit drieth the bones.

Proverbs 17:22

*T*he two most important words: "Thank you." The most important word: "We." The least important word: "I."

Don't be selfish.... Be humble, thinking of others as better than yourself.

Philippians 2:3 TLB

*H*ere's the key of success and the key to failure: we become what we think about....

Finally, brethren, whatsoever things are true,
whatsoever things are honest...if there be any virtue,
and if there be any praise, think on these things.

Philippians 4:8

*A*lways bear in mind that your own resolution to success is more important than any other one thing.

For the LORD *God will help me; therefore shall I not be confounded: therefore have I set my face like a flint, and I know that I shall not be ashamed.*

Isaiah 50:7

Triumph is just "umph" added to try.

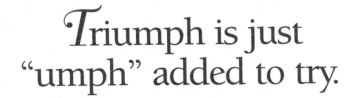

Whatsoever thy hand findeth to do, do it with thy might....

Ecclesiastes 9:10

A goal properly set is halfway reached.

And the LORD answered me, and said,
Write the vision, and make it plain upon
tables, that he may run that readeth it.

Habakkuk 2:2

I think the one lesson
I have learned is that
there is no substitute
for paying attention.

*Therefore we ought to give the more earnest
heed to the things which we have heard,
lest at any time we should let them slip.*

Hebrews 2:1

A good listener is not only popular everywhere, but after a while he knows something.

The ear that heareth the reproof of life abideth among the wise.

Proverbs 15:31

You may be disappointed if you fail, but you are doomed if you don't try.

The sluggard craves and gets nothing,
but the desires of the diligent are fully satisfied.

Proverbs 13:4 NIV

Success is never final;
failure is never fatal; it
is courage that counts.

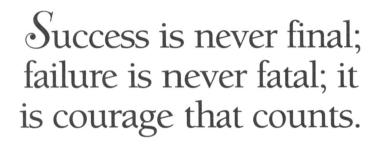

Be of good courage, and he shall strengthen
your heart, all ye that hope in the LORD.

Psalm 31:24

I count him braver
who overcomes his desires
than him who conquers
his enemies; for the
hardest victory is the
victory over self.

⊹⊱•⊰⊹

...I beat my body and make it my slave....
1 Corinthians 9:27 NIV

Vision is the world's most desperate need. There are no hopeless situations, only people who think hopelessly.

Where there is no vision, the people perish....
Proverbs 29:18

"*The* Supervisor's Prayer"
Lord when I am wrong, make
me willing to change; when I am
right, make, me easy to live with.
So strengthen me that the power
of my example will far exceed
the authority of my rank.

*...To offer ourselves as a model for you,
that you might follow our example.*

2 Thessalonians 3:9 NASB

Give me a task too big, too hard for human hands, then I shall come at length to lean on Thee, and leaning, find my strength.

Trust in the LORD with all your heart and lean not on your own understanding.

Proverbs 3:5 NIV

The most important single ingredient in the formula of success is knowing how to get along with people.

See that no one pays back evil for evil, but always try to do good to each other and to everyone else.

1 Thessalonians 5:15 TLB

Everyone thinks of changing the world, but no one thinks of changing himself.

...unless you change and become like little children you will never enter the kingdom of heaven.

Matthew 18:3 NIV

Courage is resistance to fear, mastery of fear — not absence of fear.

Yea, though I walk through the valley of the shadow of death, I will fear no evil: for thou art with me; thy rod and thy staff they comfort me.

Psalm 23:4

Prayer is an invisible tool which is wielded in a visible world.

For the weapons of our warfare are not carnal,
but mighty through God to the pulling down of strong holds.

2 Corinthians 10:4

Men will spend their health getting wealth; then, gladly pay all they have earned to get health back.

*For what will it profit a man if he gains
the whole world and forfeits his life....*

Matthew 16:26 AMP

$\mathcal{L}$et us not say, Every
man is the architect of his
own fortune; but let us say,
Every man is the architect
of his own character.

...till I die I will not remove mine integrity from me.
My righteousness I hold fast, and will not let it go:
my heart shall not reproach me so long as I live.

Job 27:5,6

*I*t is impossible for that man to despair who remembers that his Helper is omnipotent.

I will lift up my eyes to the mountains; from whence shall my help come? My help comes from the Lord, who made heaven and earth.

Psalm 121:1,2 NASB

*T*he price of success is hard work, dedication to the job at hand, and determination that whether we win or lose, we have applied the best of ourselves to the task at hand.

And whatsoever ye do, do it heartily,
as to the Lord, and not unto men.

Colossians 3:23

People, places, and things were never meant to give us life. God alone is the author of a fulfilling life.

...I am come that they might have life,
and that they might have it more abundantly.

John 10:10

Common Courtesies
For Graduates Section

And just as you want people to treat you,
treat them in the same way.

Luke 6:31 NASB

So then, while we have opportunity,
let us do good to all men. . . .

Galatians 6:10 NIV

*A*lways say thank-you,
excuse me and please
when you have done a
favor or when you are
apologizing.

*And just as you want people to treat you,
treat them in the same way.*

Luke 6:31 NASB

Always knock and ask permission before entering someone's room.

So then, while we have opportunity,
let us do good to all men....
Galatians 6:10 NIV

Don't put your feet up on the furniture. Feet do not enhance the look of the desk or the table.

And just as you want people to treat you, treat them in the same way.

Luke 6:31 NASB

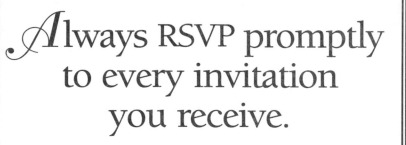

*A*lways RSVP promptly
to every invitation
you receive.

So then, while we have opportunity,
let us do good to all men....
Galatians 6:10 NIV

Return anything borrowed on time, and in good condition.

*And just as you want people to treat you,
treat them in the same way.*

Luke 6:31 NASB

Be on time for appointments; leave on time, too, for nothing is more boring than someone who overstays his welcome.

So then, while we have opportunity, let us do good to all men....

Galatians 6:10 NIV

When you dial a wrong number, say, "I'm sorry, excuse me" — instead of slamming down the receiver in the other person's ear.

And just as you want people to treat you, treat them in the same way.

Luke 6:31 NASB

Never cheat on your place in line.

*So then, while we have opportunity,
let us do good to all men....*

Galatians 6:10 NIV

Show respect to anyone in authority.

And just as you want people to treat you,
treat them in the same way.

Luke 6:31 NASB

Drive your car carefully, not only out of consideration for others but also to save lives.

*So then, while we have opportunity,
let us do good to all men....*

Galatians 6:10 NIV

Learn how to pay compliments. Start with the members of your family, and you will find it will become easier later in life to compliment others. It's a great asset.

And just as you want people to treat you, treat them in the same way.

Luke 6:31 NASB